MW00436666

Gates of Prayer
for Weekdays and
at a House of Mourning

תְּפִלּוֹת לְחוֹל
וּבְבֵית הָאָבֵל

A Gender Sensitive Prayerbook

Chaim Stern, Editor

CENTRAL CONFERENCE OF AMERICAN RABBIS
1992

ON USAGE

The following typographic conventions are used in this prayerbook. They are suggestions only, and congregations should feel free to follow their own *minhagim*.

The roman typestyle is used whenever we suggest the English be read by the person leading the service.

> *Paragraphs set in italics and indented might be read in English by the congregation as a whole. In congregations where unison reading is not the norm, such passages may be read by diverse individuals.*

Smaller roman type is used for passages which might be chanted or sung—generally in Hebrew.

San serif type is used for transliterations.

° The open circle signifies that the English is a variation on the theme of—rather than a translation of—the Hebrew.

■ The solid box is used for footnotes.

* Asterisks mark insertions for special occasions.

＿ indicates a *kamatz katan*.
＇

The Central Conference of American Rabbis expresses its warm gratitude to Rabbi A. Stanley Dreyfus for his meticulous copy editing of this volume.

ISBN: 0-88123-039-1 $2.50 *(Heb. opening)*   0-88123-041-3 $2.50 *(Eng. opening)*

Designed by Barry Nostradamus Sher. Composed at Nostradamus Advertising by Warren Wolfsohn. Hebrew set in NewHebrew, developed by Warren Wolfsohn from Hadassah (Davka Corporation) and Hebraica (Linguist's Software, Inc.).

Copyright © 1992, Central Conference of American Rabbis. All Rights Reserved.
99 98 97 96   10 9 8 7 6 5

CONTENTS

Ashrei אשרי

אַשְׁרֵי יוֹשְׁבֵי בֵיתֶךָ; עוֹד יְהַלְלוּךָ סֶּלָה.
אַשְׁרֵי הָעָם שֶׁכָּכָה לּוֹ; אַשְׁרֵי הָעָם שֶׁיהוה אֱלֹהָיו.

Happy are those who dwell in Your house;

they will sing your praise for ever.

Happy the people to whom such blessing falls;

Happy the people of the Eternal God.

Psalm 145

תְּהִלָּה לְדָוִד.
אֲרוֹמִמְךָ, אֱלוֹהַי הַמֶּלֶךְ, וַאֲבָרְכָה שִׁמְךָ לְעוֹלָם וָעֶד.
בְּכָל־יוֹם אֲבָרְכֶךָ, וַאֲהַלְלָה שִׁמְךָ לְעוֹלָם וָעֶד.

I will exalt You, my Sovereign God,

I will praise Your name for ever.

Every day I will praise You;

I will extol Your name for ever.

גָּדוֹל יהוה וּמְהֻלָּל מְאֹד, וְלִגְדֻלָּתוֹ אֵין חֵקֶר.
דּוֹר לְדוֹר יְשַׁבַּח מַעֲשֶׂיךָ, וּגְבוּרֹתֶיךָ יַגִּידוּ.

Great are You, Eternal One, and worthy of praise;

and infinite is Your greatness.

Several verses of this psalm are translated into second person, to
maintain gender-neutrality in the English text

One generation shall acclaim Your work to the next;
> *they shall tell of Your mighty acts.*

הֲדַר כְּבוֹד הוֹדֶֽךָ, וְדִבְרֵי נִפְלְאוֹתֶֽיךָ אָשִֽׂיחָה.
וֶעֱזוּז נוֹרְאוֹתֶֽיךָ יֹאמֵֽרוּ, וּגְדֻלָּתְךָ אֲסַפְּרֶֽנָּה.

They shall bring word of Your radiant glory;
> *and bear witness to Your wondrous works.*

They shall speak of Your awesome might,
> *and make known Your greatness.*

זֵֽכֶר רַב־טוּבְךָ יַבִּֽיעוּ, וְצִדְקָתְךָ יְרַנֵּֽנוּ.
חַנּוּן וְרַחוּם יהוה, אֶֽרֶךְ אַפַּֽיִם וּגְדָל־חָֽסֶד.
טוֹב־יהוה לַכֹּל, וְרַחֲמָיו עַל־כָּל־מַעֲשָׂיו.

They shall tell the world of Your goodness,
> *and sing of Your righteousness.*

"God is gracious and compassionate,
endlessly patient, overflowing with love."
> *"You are good to all; Your compassion*
> *shelters all Your creatures."*

יוֹדֽוּךָ יהוה כָּל מַעֲשֶֽׂיךָ, וַחֲסִידֶֽיךָ יְבָרְכֽוּכָה.
כְּבוֹד מַלְכוּתְךָ יֹאמֵֽרוּ, וּגְבוּרָתְךָ יְדַבֵּֽרוּ.

All Your works shall glorify You;
> *Your faithful ones shall praise You.*

They shall proclaim Your majestic glory,
> *they shall tell of Your might:*

לְהוֹדִֽיעַ לִבְנֵי הָאָדָם גְּבוּרֹתָיו, וּכְבוֹד הֲדַר מַלְכוּתוֹ.
מַלְכוּתְךָ מַלְכוּת כָּל־עֹלָמִים, וּמֶמְשַׁלְתְּךָ בְּכָל־דּוֹר וָדוֹר.

to reveal Your power to the world,

and the glorious splendor of Your rule.

You are sovereign to the end of time;

You reign through all generations.

סוֹמֵךְ יהוה לְכָל־הַנֹּפְלִים, וְזוֹקֵף לְכָל־הַכְּפוּפִים.
עֵינֵי־כֹל אֵלֶיךָ יְשַׂבֵּרוּ, וְאַתָּה נוֹתֵן־לָהֶם אֶת־אָכְלָם בְּעִתּוֹ.

You support the falling, Eternal One;

You raise up all who are bowed down.

The eyes of all are turned to You;

You sustain them in time of need.

פּוֹתֵחַ אֶת־יָדֶךָ וּמַשְׂבִּיעַ לְכָל־חַי רָצוֹן.
צַדִּיק יהוה בְּכָל־דְּרָכָיו, וְחָסִיד בְּכָל־מַעֲשָׂיו.

You open Your hand,

to fulfill the needs of all the living.

You are just in all Your ways,

loving in all Your deeds.

קָרוֹב יהוה לְכָל־קֹרְאָיו, לְכֹל אֲשֶׁר יִקְרָאֻהוּ בֶאֱמֶת.
רְצוֹן־יְרֵאָיו יַעֲשֶׂה, וְאֶת־שַׁוְעָתָם יִשְׁמַע וְיוֹשִׁיעֵם.
שׁוֹמֵר יהוה אֶת־כָּל־אֹהֲבָיו, וְאֵת כָּל־הָרְשָׁעִים יַשְׁמִיד.

You are near to all who call upon You,

to all who call upon You in truth:

You fulfill the hope of all who revere You;

You hear their cry and help them.

7

תְּהִלַּת יהוה יְדַבֶּר־פִּי וִיבָרֵךְ כָּל־בָּשָׂר שֵׁם קָדְשׁוֹ לְעוֹלָם
וָעֶד.
וַאֲנַחְנוּ נְבָרֵךְ יָה מֵעַתָּה וְעַד־עוֹלָם. הַלְלוּיָהּ.

My lips shall declare the glory of God;
let all flesh praise Your holy name for ever and ever.

We will praise Your name now and always. Halleluyah!

All rise

READER'S KADDISH   חצי קדיש

יִתְגַּדַּל וְיִתְקַדַּשׁ שְׁמֵהּ רַבָּא בְּעָלְמָא דִי־בְרָא כִרְעוּתֵהּ,
וְיַמְלִיךְ מַלְכוּתֵהּ בְּחַיֵּיכוֹן וּבְיוֹמֵיכוֹן וּבְחַיֵּי דְכָל־בֵּית
יִשְׂרָאֵל, בַּעֲגָלָא וּבִזְמַן קָרִיב, וְאִמְרוּ: אָמֵן.

יְהֵא שְׁמֵהּ רַבָּא מְבָרַךְ לְעָלַם וּלְעָלְמֵי עָלְמַיָּא.

יִתְבָּרַךְ וְיִשְׁתַּבַּח, וְיִתְפָּאַר וְיִתְרוֹמַם וְיִתְנַשֵּׂא, וְיִתְהַדָּר
וְיִתְעַלֶּה וְיִתְהַלָּל שְׁמֵהּ דְּקוּדְשָׁא, בְּרִיךְ הוּא, לְעֵלָּא
מִן־כָּל־בִּרְכָתָא וְשִׁירָתָא, תֻּשְׁבְּחָתָא וְנֶחֱמָתָא דַּאֲמִירָן
בְּעָלְמָא, וְאִמְרוּ: אָמֵן.

Yit-ga-dal v'yit-ka-dash sh'mei ra-ba b'al-ma di-v'ra chir-u-tei,
v'yam-lich mal-chu-tei b'cha-yei-chon u-v'yo-mei-chon u-v'cha-yei
d'chol beit Yis-ra-eil, ba-a-ga-la u-viz-man ka-riv, v'im'ru: A-mein.

Y'hei sh'mei ra-ba m'va-rach l'a-lam u-l'al-mei al-ma-ya.

Yit-ba-rach v'yish-ta-bach v'yit-pa-ar, v'yit-ro-mam, v'yit-na-sei, v'yit-
ha-dar, v'yit-a-leh, v'yit-ha-lal sh'mei d'kud-sha, b'rich hu, l'ei-la min
kol bir-cha-ta v'shi-ra-ta, tush-b'cha-ta v'neh-cheh-ma-ta da-a-mi-
ran b'al-ma, v'im'ru: A-mein.

Let the glory of God be extolled, and God's great name be hallowed in the
world whose creation God willed. May God rule in our own day, in our
own lives, and in the life of all Israel, and let us say: Amen.

Let God's great name be blessed for ever and ever.

Beyond all the praises, songs, and adorations that we can utter is the Holy One, the Blessed One, whom yet we glorify, honor, and exalt. And let us say: Amen.

תפלה T'filah

אֲדֹנָי שְׂפָתַי תִּפְתָּח וּפִי יַגִּיד תְּהִלָּתֶךָ:

Eternal God, open my lips, that my mouth may declare Your glory.

GOD OF ALL GENERATIONS   אבות ואמהות

בָּרוּךְ אַתָּה יְיָ, אֱלֹהֵינוּ וֵאלֹהֵי אֲבוֹתֵינוּ וְאִמּוֹתֵינוּ:
אֱלֹהֵי אַבְרָהָם, אֱלֹהֵי יִצְחָק, וֵאלֹהֵי יַעֲקֹב.
אֱלֹהֵי שָׂרָה, אֱלֹהֵי רִבְקָה, אֱלֹהֵי לֵאָה, וֵאלֹהֵי רָחֵל.
הָאֵל הַגָּדוֹל הַגִּבּוֹר וְהַנּוֹרָא, אֵל עֶלְיוֹן, גּוֹמֵל חֲסָדִים
טוֹבִים וְקוֹנֵה הַכֹּל, וְזוֹכֵר חַסְדֵי אָבוֹת וְאִמָּהוֹת,
וּמֵבִיא גְאֻלָּה לִבְנֵי בְנֵיהֶם, לְמַעַן שְׁמוֹ בְּאַהֲבָה.

BETWEEN ROSH HASHANAH AND YOM KIPPUR ADD:

זָכְרֵנוּ לְחַיִּים, מֶלֶךְ חָפֵץ בַּחַיִּים,
וְכָתְבֵנוּ בְּסֵפֶר הַחַיִּים, לְמַעַנְךָ אֱלֹהִים חַיִּים.

מֶלֶךְ עוֹזֵר וּמוֹשִׁיעַ וּמָגֵן.
בָּרוּךְ אַתָּה יְיָ, מָגֵן אַבְרָהָם וְעֶזְרַת שָׂרָה.

Ba-ruch a-ta Adonai, Eh-lo-hei-nu vei-lo-hei a-vo-tei-nu v'i-mo-tei-nu: Eh-lo-hei Av-ra-ham, eh-lo-hei Yitz-chak, vei-lo-hei Ya-a-kov. Eh-lo-hei Sa-rah, eh-lo-hei Riv-kah, eh-lo-hei Lei-ah, vei-lo-hei Ra-cheil. Ha-eil ha-ga-dol ha-gi-bor v'ha-no-ra, eil el-yon. Go-meil cha-sa-dim toh-vim, v'ko-nei ha-kol, v'zo-cheir chas-dei a-voht v'i-ma-hoht, u-mei-vi g'u-la li-v'nei v'nei-hem, l'ma-an sh'mo, b'a-ha-va.

Zoch'rei-nu l'cha-yim, meh-lech cha-feitz ba-cha-yim, v'cho-t'vei-nu
ba-sei-fer ha-cha-yim, l'ma-an-cha Eh-lo-him cha-yim.

Meh-lech o-zeir u-mo-shi-a u-ma-gein.
Ba-ruch a-ta Adonai, ma-gein Av-ra-ham v'ez-rat Sa-rah.

°God of ages past and future, God of this day,
as You were with our mothers and fathers, be with us as well.

> *As You strengthened them, strengthen us.*

As you were their Guide, be ours as well.

> *Grant that we too may be bearers of Your teaching,*
> *teachers of Your truth.*

Then our tradition shall endure, and Israel live;
from mother and father to daughter and son,
and all who follow them.

> *May students of Torah become teachers,*
> *that the people and its tradition endure.*
> *The people and its tradition will live.*

GOD'S POWER   גבורות

אַתָּה גִבּוֹר לְעוֹלָם, אֲדֹנָי, מְחַיֵּה הַכֹּל אַתָּה, רַב לְהוֹשִׁיעַ.
מְכַלְכֵּל חַיִּים בְּחֶסֶד, מְחַיֵּה הַכֹּל בְּרַחֲמִים רַבִּים. סוֹמֵךְ
נוֹפְלִים, וְרוֹפֵא חוֹלִים, וּמַתִּיר אֲסוּרִים, וּמְקַיֵּם אֱמוּנָתוֹ
לִישֵׁנֵי עָפָר. מִי כָמוֹךָ בַּעַל גְּבוּרוֹת, וּמִי דוֹמֶה לָךְ, מֶלֶךְ
מֵמִית וּמְחַיֵּה וּמַצְמִיחַ יְשׁוּעָה?

מִי כָמוֹךָ, אֵל הָרַחֲמִים, זוֹכֵר יְצוּרָיו לְחַיִּים בְּרַחֲמִים?

וְנֶאֱמָן אַתָּה לְהַחֲיוֹת הַכֹּל. בָּרוּךְ אַתָּה יְיָ, מְחַיֵּה הַכֹּל.

A-ta gi-bor l'o-lam, Adonai, m'cha-yei ha-kol a-ta, rav l'ho-shi-a.
M'chal-keil cha-yim b'cheh-sed, m'cha-yei ha-kol b'ra-cha-mim ra-
bim. So-meich no-f'lim, v'ro-fei cho-lim, u-ma-tir a-su-rim, u-m'ka-
yeim eh-mu-na-toh li-shei-nei a-far. Mi cha-mo-cha ba-al g'vu-roht,
u-mi doh-meh lach, meh-lech mei-mit u-m'cha-yeh u-matz-mi-ach
y'shu-a?

BETWEEN ROSH HASHANAH AND YOM KIPPUR ADD:

Mi cha-mo-cha, eil ha-ra-cha-mim, zo-cheir y'tzu-rav l'cha-yim
b'ra-cha-mim?

V'neh-eh-man a-ta l'ha-cha-yoht ha-kol, Ba-ruch a-ta Adonai,
m'cha-yei ha-kol.

°Your might, O God, is everlasting;

Help us to use our strength for good.

You are the Source of life and blessing;

Help us to choose life for ourselves and our children.

You are the Support of the falling;

Help us to lift up the fallen.

You are the Author of freedom;

Help us to set free the captive;

You are our Hope in death as in life;

Help us to keep faith with those who sleep in the dust.

Your might, O God, is everlasting;

Help us to use our strength for good.

SANCTIFICATION קדושה

נְקַדֵּשׁ אֶת־שִׁמְךָ בָּעוֹלָם, כְּשֵׁם שֶׁמַּקְדִּישִׁים אוֹתוֹ בִּשְׁמֵי
מָרוֹם, כַּכָּתוּב עַל־יַד נְבִיאֶךָ: וְקָרָא זֶה אֶל־זֶה וְאָמַר:

We sanctify Your name on earth, even as all things, to the ends
of time and space, proclaim Your holiness, and in the words of
the prophet we say:

קָדוֹשׁ, קָדוֹשׁ, קָדוֹשׁ יהוה צְבָאוֹת,
מְלֹא כָל־הָאָרֶץ כְּבוֹדוֹ.

Ka-dosh, ka-dosh, ka-dosh Adonai tz'va-oht,
m'lo chol ha-a-retz k'vo-doh.

Holy, holy, holy is the Eternal One, God of the Hosts of Heaven!
The whole earth is ablaze with Your glory!

לְעֻמָּתָם בָּרוּךְ יֹאמֵרוּ:

All being recounts Your praise:

בָּרוּךְ כְּבוֹד־יהוה מִמְּקוֹמוֹ.

Ba-ruch k'vod Adonai mim-ko-mo.

Praised be the glory of God in heaven and earth.

וּבְדִבְרֵי קָדְשְׁךָ כָּתוּב לֵאמֹר:

And this is Your sacred word:

יִמְלֹךְ יהוה לְעוֹלָם, אֱלֹהַיִךְ צִיּוֹן, לְדֹר וָדֹר. הַלְלוּיָהּ!

Yim-loch Adonai l'o-lam, eh-lo-ha-yich tzi-yon,
l'dor va-dor. Ha-l'lu-yah!

The Eternal One shall reign for ever; your God, O Zion, from
generation to generation. Halleluyah!

12

לְדוֹר וָדוֹר נַגִּיד גָּדְלֶךָ וּלְנֵצַח נְצָחִים קְדֻשָּׁתְךָ נַקְדִּישׁ. וְשִׁבְחֲךָ, אֱלֹהֵינוּ, מִפִּינוּ לֹא יָמוּשׁ לְעוֹלָם וָעֶד. *בָּרוּךְ אַתָּה יְיָ, הָאֵל הַקָּדוֹשׁ.

*BETWEEN ROSH HASHANAH AND YOM KIPPUR CONCLUDE:

בָּרוּךְ אַתָּה יְיָ, הַמֶּלֶךְ הַקָּדוֹשׁ.

To all generations we will make known Your greatness, and to all eternity proclaim Your holiness. Your praise, O God, shall never depart from our lips.

*We praise You, Eternal One, the holy God.

*BETWEEN ROSH HASHANAH AND YOM KIPPUR CONCLUDE:

We praise You, Eternal One: You rule in holiness.

All are seated

THE INTERMEDIATE BLESSINGS   בקשות

We give thanks for the divine flame that glows within, the gift of reason that enables us to search after knowledge.

Blessed is the Eternal Source of wisdom and knowledge.

May our pride of intellect never be an idol turning us away from feeling wonder and awe. And as we grow in knowledge, may we remain aware that all our knowledge is but a handful of bright pebbles picked from the wide shore of the unknown.

Blessed is the One to whom all things are known.

May the beauty and mystery of the world move us to reverence and humility. Let the tree of knowledge bear good fruit for us and our children.

Blessed is the One from whom all blessings flow.

And let the consciousness of Your presence be the glory of our lives, making joyous our days and years.

Blessed is the One who hearkens to prayer.

❖ ❖

MEDITATION

❖ ❖

יִהְיוּ לְרָצוֹן אִמְרֵי־פִי וְהֶגְיוֹן לִבִּי לְפָנֶיךָ, יהוה, צוּרִי וְגֹאֲלִי.

May the words of my mouth, and the meditations of my heart,
be acceptable to You, O God, my Rock and my Redeemer.

❖

עֹשֶׂה שָׁלוֹם בִּמְרוֹמָיו, הוּא יַעֲשֶׂה שָׁלוֹם עָלֵינוּ וְעַל־כָּל־
יִשְׂרָאֵל, וְאִמְרוּ: אָמֵן.

O-seh sha-lom bim-ro-mav, hu ya-a-seh sha-lom a-lei-nu v'al kol
Yis-ra-eil, v'im-ru: A-mein.

May the One who causes peace to reign in the high heavens let
peace descend on us, on all Israel, and all the world.

Prayers for the House of Mourning begin on page 37
Aleinu is on page 41

Evening Service ערבית לחול

"And after the fire, a still, small voice." *(I Kings 19)*

You give meaning to our days, to our struggles and strivings. In the stillness of the night and in the press of the crowd, Yours is the voice within that brings joy and peace.

We do not ask for a life of ease, for happiness without alloy. We ask only to be uncomplaining and unafraid. In our darkness be our light, and in our loneliness help us discover the many souls akin to our own. Give us strength to face life with courage, to draw blessing even from its discords and conflicts. Make us understand that life calls us not merely to enjoy the richness of the earth, but to exult in heights gained after the toil of climbing.

Let our darkness be dispelled by Your love, that we may rise above fear and failure, our steps sustained by faith. You give meaning to our days; You are our support and our trust.

All rise

The Sh'ma and Its Blessings שמע וברכותיה

בָּרְכוּ אֶת־יְיָ הַמְבֹרָךְ!

Praise the One to whom praise is due!

בָּרוּךְ יְיָ הַמְבֹרָךְ לְעוֹלָם וָעֶד!

Ba-ruch Adonai ha-m'vo-rach l'o-lam va-ed!

Praised be the One to whom praise is due, now and for ever!

15

CREATION מעריב ערבים

בָּרוּךְ אַתָּה יְיָ, אֱלֹהֵינוּ מֶלֶךְ הָעוֹלָם, אֲשֶׁר בִּדְבָרוֹ
מַעֲרִיב עֲרָבִים, בְּחׇכְמָה פּוֹתֵחַ שְׁעָרִים, וּבִתְבוּנָה מְשַׁנֶּה
עִתִּים, וּמַחֲלִיף אֶת־הַזְּמַנִּים, וּמְסַדֵּר אֶת־הַכּוֹכָבִים
בְּמִשְׁמְרוֹתֵיהֶם בָּרָקִיעַ כִּרְצוֹנוֹ.

בּוֹרֵא יוֹם וָלַיְלָה, גּוֹלֵל אוֹר מִפְּנֵי חֹשֶׁךְ וְחֹשֶׁךְ מִפְּנֵי אוֹר,
וּמַעֲבִיר יוֹם וּמֵבִיא לָיְלָה, וּמַבְדִּיל בֵּין יוֹם וּבֵין לָיְלָה,
יְיָ צְבָאוֹת שְׁמוֹ. אֵל חַי וְקַיָּם, תָּמִיד יִמְלוֹךְ עָלֵינוּ,
לְעוֹלָם וָעֶד. בָּרוּךְ אַתָּה יְיָ, הַמַּעֲרִיב עֲרָבִים.

Praised be our Eternal God, Ruler of the universe, whose word
brings on the evening, whose wisdom opens heaven's gates,
whose understanding makes the ages pass and the seasons
alternate, and whose will controls the stars as they travel
through the skies.

You are Creator of day and night, rolling light away from
darkness, and darkness from light; You cause day to pass
and bring on the night; separating day from night; You
command the Hosts of Heaven! May the living and eternal
God rule us always, to the end of time! We praise You,
Eternal One, whose word makes evening fall.

REVELATION אהבת עולם

אַהֲבַת עוֹלָם בֵּית יִשְׂרָאֵל עַמְּךָ אָהָבְתָּ.
תּוֹרָה וּמִצְוֹת, חֻקִּים וּמִשְׁפָּטִים אוֹתָנוּ לִמַּדְתָּ.

עַל־כֵּן, יְיָ אֱלֹהֵינוּ, בְּשָׁכְבֵּנוּ וּבְקוּמֵנוּ נָשִׂיחַ בְּחֻקֶּיךָ,
וְנִשְׂמַח בְּדִבְרֵי תוֹרָתֶךָ וּבְמִצְוֹתֶיךָ לְעוֹלָם וָעֶד.

כִּי הֵם חַיֵּינוּ וְאֹרֶךְ יָמֵינוּ, וּבָהֶם נֶהְגֶּה יוֹמָם וָלָיְלָה.
וְאַהֲבָתְךָ אַל־תָּסוּר מִמֶּנּוּ לְעוֹלָמִים!

בָּרוּךְ אַתָּה יְיָ, אוֹהֵב עַמּוֹ יִשְׂרָאֵל.

Unending is Your love for Your people, the House of Israel:
Torah and Mitzvot, laws and precepts have You taught us.

Therefore, O God, when we lie down and when we rise up, we
will meditate on Your laws and rejoice in Your Torah and
Mitzvot for ever.

*Day and night we will reflect on them, for they are our
life and the length of our days. Then Your love shall
never depart from our hearts! We praise You, Eternal
One, who love Your people Israel.*

שְׁמַע יִשְׂרָאֵל: יהוה אֱלֹהֵינוּ יהוה אֶחָד׀

Sh'ma Yis-ra-eil: Adonai Eh-lo-hei-nu, Adonai Eh-chad!

Hear, O Israel: the Eternal One is our God,
the Eternal God alone!

בָּרוּךְ שֵׁם כְּבוֹד מַלְכוּתוֹ לְעוֹלָם וָעֶד׀

Ba-ruch sheim k'vod mal-chu-toh l'o-lam va-ed!

Blessed is God's glorious majesty for ever and ever!

All are seated

וְאָהַבְתָּ אֵת יְהֹוָה אֱלֹהֶיךָ בְּכָל־לְבָבְךָ וּבְכָל־נַפְשְׁךָ
וּבְכָל־מְאֹדֶךָ: וְהָיוּ הַדְּבָרִים הָאֵלֶּה אֲשֶׁר אָנֹכִי מְצַוְּךָ
הַיּוֹם עַל־לְבָבֶךָ: וְשִׁנַּנְתָּם לְבָנֶיךָ וְדִבַּרְתָּ בָּם בְּשִׁבְתְּךָ
בְּבֵיתֶךָ וּבְלֶכְתְּךָ בַדֶּרֶךְ וּבְשָׁכְבְּךָ וּבְקוּמֶךָ: וּקְשַׁרְתָּם
לְאוֹת עַל־יָדֶךָ וְהָיוּ לְטֹטָפֹת בֵּין עֵינֶיךָ: וּכְתַבְתָּם
עַל־מְזֻזֹת בֵּיתֶךָ וּבִשְׁעָרֶיךָ:

17

V'a-hav-ta et Adonai eh-lo-heh-cha b'chol l'va-v'cha u-v'chol naf-
sh'cha u-v'chol m'o-deh-cha. V'ha-yu ha-d'va-rim ha-ei-leh a-sher
a-no-chi m'tza-v'cha ha-yom al l'va-veh-cha. V'shi-nan-tam l'va-neh-
cha v'di-bar-ta bam b'shiv-t'cha b'vei-teh-cha u-v'lech-t'cha va-deh-
rech u-v'shoch-b'cha u-v'ku-meh-cha. U-k'shar-tam l'oht al ya-deh-
cha v'ha-yu l'toh-ta-foht bein ei-neh-cha; u-ch'tav-tam al m'zu-zoht
bei-teh-cha u-vi-sh'a-reh-cha.

> *You shall love the Eternal One, your God, with all your
> heart, with all your mind, with all your being. Set these
> words, which I command you this day, upon your heart.
> Teach them faithfully to your children; speak of them in
> your home and on your way, when you lie down and when
> you rise up. Bind them as a sign upon your hand; let them
> be a symbol before your eyes; inscribe them on the door-
> posts of your house, and on your gates.*

לְמַעַן תִּזְכְּרוּ וַעֲשִׂיתֶם אֶת־כָּל־מִצְוֹתָי וִהְיִיתֶם קְדֹשִׁים
לֵאלֹהֵיכֶם: אֲנִי יהוה אֱלֹהֵיכֶם אֲשֶׁר הוֹצֵאתִי אֶתְכֶם
מֵאֶרֶץ מִצְרַיִם לִהְיוֹת לָכֶם לֵאלֹהִים אֲנִי יהוה אֱלֹהֵיכֶם:

L'ma-an tiz-k'ru va-a-si-tem et kol mitz-vo-tai, vi-h'yi-tem k'doh-
shim lei-lo-hei-chem. A-ni Adonai eh-lo-hei-chem a-sher ho-tzei-ti
et-chem mei-eh-retz mitz-ra-yim li-h'yoht la-chem lei-lo-him. A-ni
Adonai eh-lo-hei-chem.

> *Be mindful of all My Mitzvot, and do them: so shall you
> consecrate yourselves to your God. I am your Eternal God
> who led you out of Egypt to be your God; I am your
> Eternal God.*

REDEMPTION   גאולה

אֱמֶת וֶאֱמוּנָה כָּל־זֹאת, וְקַיָּם עָלֵינוּ כִּי הוּא יְיָ אֱלֹהֵינוּ
וְאֵין זוּלָתוֹ, וַאֲנַחְנוּ יִשְׂרָאֵל עַמּוֹ. הַפּוֹדֵנוּ מִיַּד מְלָכִים,
מַלְכֵּנוּ הַגּוֹאֲלֵנוּ מִכַּף כָּל־הֶעָרִיצִים.

הָעֹשֶׂה גְדֹלוֹת עַד אֵין חֵקֶר, וְנִפְלָאוֹת עַד־אֵין מִסְפָּר.
הַשָּׂם נַפְשֵׁנוּ בַּחַיִּים, וְלֹא־נָתַן לַמּוֹט רַגְלֵנוּ.
הָעֹשֶׂה לָּנוּ נִסִּים בְּפַרְעֹה, אוֹתוֹת וּמוֹפְתִים בְּאַדְמַת
בְּנֵי חָם. וַיּוֹצֵא אֶת־עַמּוֹ יִשְׂרָאֵל מִתּוֹכָם לְחֵרוּת עוֹלָם.
וְרָאוּ בָנָיו וּבְנוֹתָיו גְּבוּרָתוֹ; שִׁבְּחוּ וְהוֹדוּ לִשְׁמוֹ.
וּמַלְכוּתוֹ בְּרָצוֹן קִבְּלוּ עֲלֵיהֶם. מֹשֶׁה וּמִרְיָם וּבְנֵי
יִשְׂרָאֵל לְךָ עָנוּ שִׁירָה בְּשִׂמְחָה רַבָּה, וְאָמְרוּ כֻלָּם:

All this we hold to be true and sure; You alone are our God;
there is none else, and we are Israel Your people.

> *You are our Sovereign: You deliver us from the hand of*
> *oppressors, and save us from the fist of tyrants,*

You do wonders without number,
marvels that pass our understanding.

> *You give us our life; by Your help we survive*
> *all who seek our destruction.*

You did wonders for us in the land of Egypt,
miracles and marvels in the land of Pharaoh,

> *You led Your people Israel out,*
> *forever to serve You in freedom.*

When Your children witnessed Your power, they extolled You
and gave You thanks; willingly they enthroned You; and, full of
joy, Moses, Miriam, and all Israel sang this song:

מִי־כָמֹכָה בָּאֵלִם, יהוה? מִי כָּמֹכָה, נֶאְדָּר בַּקֹּדֶשׁ,
נוֹרָא תְהִלֹּת, עֹשֵׂה פֶלֶא?
מַלְכוּתְךָ רָאוּ בָנֶיךָ, בּוֹקֵעַ יָם לִפְנֵי מֹשֶׁה; זֶה אֵלִי!
עָנוּ וְאָמְרוּ: יהוה יִמְלֹךְ לְעֹלָם וָעֶד!

וְנֶאֱמַר: כִּי פָדָה יְיָ אֶת־יַעֲקֹב, וּגְאָלוֹ מִיַּד חָזָק
מִמֶּנּוּ. בָּרוּךְ אַתָּה יְיָ, גָּאַל יִשְׂרָאֵל.

19

Mi cha-mo-cha ba-ei-lim, Adonai? Mi ka-mo-cha, neh-dar ba-ko-desh, no-ra t'hi-loht, o-sei feh-leh?

Mal-chu-t'cha ra-u va-neh-cha, bo-kei-a yam lif-nei Mo-sheh; zeh ei-li! a-nu v'am-ru: Adonai yim-loch l'o-lam va-ed.

V'neh-eh-mar: Ki fa-da Adonai et Ya-a-kov, u-g'a-lo mi-yad cha-zak mi-meh-nu. Ba-ruch a-ta Adonai, ga-al Yis-ra-eil.

Who is like You, Eternal One, among the gods that are worshipped? Who is like You, majestic in holiness, awesome in splendor, doing wonders?

In their escape from the sea, Your children saw Your sovereign might displayed. "This is my God!" they cried. "The Eternal will reign for ever and ever!"

And it has been said: The Eternal One delivered Jacob, and redeemed us from the hand of one stronger than ourselves. We praise You, Eternal One, Redeemer of Israel.

DIVINE PROVIDENCE   השכיבנו

הַשְׁכִּיבֵנוּ, יְיָ אֱלֹהֵינוּ, לְשָׁלוֹם, וְהַעֲמִידֵנוּ, מַלְכֵּנוּ, לְחַיִּים.
וּפְרוֹשׂ עָלֵינוּ סֻכַּת שְׁלוֹמֶךָ, וְתַקְּנֵנוּ בְּעֵצָה טוֹבָה מִלְּפָנֶיךָ,
וְהוֹשִׁיעֵנוּ לְמַעַן שְׁמֶךָ, וְהָגֵן בַּעֲדֵנוּ. וְהָסֵר מֵעָלֵינוּ אוֹיֵב,
דֶּבֶר וְחֶרֶב וְרָעָב וְיָגוֹן; וְהָסֵר שָׂטָן מִלְּפָנֵינוּ וּמֵאַחֲרֵינוּ,
וּבְצֵל כְּנָפֶיךָ תַּסְתִּירֵנוּ, כִּי אֵל שׁוֹמְרֵנוּ וּמַצִּילֵנוּ אָתָּה,
כִּי אֵל מֶלֶךְ חַנּוּן וְרַחוּם אָתָּה. וּשְׁמוֹר צֵאתֵנוּ
וּבוֹאֵנוּ לְחַיִּים וּלְשָׁלוֹם, מֵעַתָּה וְעַד עוֹלָם.

בָּרוּךְ אַתָּה יְיָ, שׁוֹמֵר עַמּוֹ יִשְׂרָאֵל לָעַד.

Grant that we may lie down in peace, Eternal God, and raise us up, O Sovereign, to life renewed. Spread over us the shelter of Your peace; guide us with Your good counsel; and for Your name's sake, be our Help.

Shield us from hatred and plague; keep us from war and famine and anguish; subdue our inclination to evil. O God,

our Guardian and Helper, our gracious and merciful Ruler,
give us refuge in the shadow of Your wings. O guard our
coming and our going, that now and always we have life
and peace.

We praise You, Eternal One, the Guardian of Israel.

All rise

READER'S KADDISH   חֲצִי קַדִּישׁ

יִתְגַּדַּל וְיִתְקַדַּשׁ שְׁמֵהּ רַבָּא בְּעָלְמָא דִּי־בְרָא כִרְעוּתֵהּ,
וְיַמְלִיךְ מַלְכוּתֵהּ בְּחַיֵּיכוֹן וּבְיוֹמֵיכוֹן וּבְחַיֵּי דְכָל־בֵּית
יִשְׂרָאֵל, בַּעֲגָלָא וּבִזְמַן קָרִיב, וְאִמְרוּ: אָמֵן.

יְהֵא שְׁמֵהּ רַבָּא מְבָרַךְ לְעָלַם וּלְעָלְמֵי עָלְמַיָּא.

יִתְבָּרַךְ וְיִשְׁתַּבַּח, וְיִתְפָּאַר וְיִתְרוֹמַם וְיִתְנַשֵּׂא, וְיִתְהַדָּר
וְיִתְעַלֶּה וְיִתְהַלָּל שְׁמֵהּ דְּקוּדְשָׁא, בְּרִיךְ הוּא, לְעֵלָּא
מִן־כָּל־בִּרְכָתָא וְשִׁירָתָא, תֻּשְׁבְּחָתָא וְנֶחֱמָתָא
דַּאֲמִירָן בְּעָלְמָא, וְאִמְרוּ: אָמֵן.

Yit-ga-dal v'yit-ka-dash sh'mei ra-ba b'al-ma di-v'ra chir-u-tei,
v'yam-lich mal-chu-tei b'cha-yei-chon u-v'yo-mei-chon u-v'cha-yei
d'chol beit Yis-ra-eil, ba-a-ga-la u-viz-man ka-riv, v'im'ru: A-mein.

Y'hei sh'mei ra-ba m'va-rach l'a-lam u-l'al-mei al-ma-ya.

Yit-ba-rach v'yish-ta-bach v'yit-pa-ar, v'yit-ro-mam, v'yit-na-sei, v'yit-
ha-dar, v'yit-a-leh, v'yit-ha-lal sh'mei d'kud'sha, b'rich hu, l'ei-la min
kol bir-cha-ta v'shi-ra-ta, tush-b'cha-ta v'neh-cheh-ma-ta da-a-mi-
ran b'al-ma, v'im'ru: A-mein.

Let the glory of God be extolled, and God's great name be hallowed in the world whose creation God willed. May God rule in our own day, in our own lives, and in the life of all Israel, and let us say: Amen.

Let God's great name be blessed for ever and ever.

Beyond all the praises, songs, and adorations that we can utter is the Holy One, the Blessed One, whom yet we glorify, honor, and exalt. And let us say: Amen.

T'filah תפלה

אֲדֹנָי שְׂפָתַי תִּפְתָּח וּפִי יַגִּיד תְּהִלָּתֶךָ:

Eternal God, open my lips, that my mouth may declare Your glory.

GOD OF ALL GENERATIONS   אבות ואמהות

בָּרוּךְ אַתָּה יְיָ, אֱלֹהֵינוּ וֵאלֹהֵי אֲבוֹתֵינוּ וְאִמּוֹתֵינוּ:
אֱלֹהֵי אַבְרָהָם, אֱלֹהֵי יִצְחָק, וֵאלֹהֵי יַעֲקֹב.
אֱלֹהֵי שָׂרָה, אֱלֹהֵי רִבְקָה, אֱלֹהֵי לֵאָה, וֵאלֹהֵי רָחֵל.
הָאֵל הַגָּדוֹל הַגִּבּוֹר וְהַנּוֹרָא, אֵל עֶלְיוֹן, גּוֹמֵל חֲסָדִים
טוֹבִים וְקוֹנֵה הַכֹּל, וְזוֹכֵר חַסְדֵי אָבוֹת וְאִמָּהוֹת,
וּמֵבִיא גְאֻלָּה לִבְנֵי בְנֵיהֶם, לְמַעַן שְׁמוֹ בְּאַהֲבָה.

BETWEEN ROSH HASHANAH AND YOM KIPPUR ADD:
זָכְרֵנוּ לְחַיִּים, מֶלֶךְ חָפֵץ בַּחַיִּים,
וְכָתְבֵנוּ בְּסֵפֶר הַחַיִּים, לְמַעַנְךָ אֱלֹהִים חַיִּים.

מֶלֶךְ עוֹזֵר וּמוֹשִׁיעַ וּמָגֵן.
בָּרוּךְ אַתָּה יְיָ, מָגֵן אַבְרָהָם וְעֶזְרַת שָׂרָה.

22

Ba-ruch a-ta Adonai, Eh-lo-hei-nu vei-lo-hei a-vo-tei-nu v'i-mo-tei-nu: Eh-lo-hei Av-ra-ham, eh-lo-hei Yitz-chak, vei-lo-hei Ya-a-kov. Eh-lo-hei Sa-rah, eh-lo-hei Riv-kah, eh-lo-hei Lei-ah, vei-lo-hei Ra-cheil. Ha-eil ha-ga-dol ha-gi-bor v'ha-no-ra, eil el-yon. Go-meil cha-sa-dim toh-vim, v'ko-nei ha-kol, v'zo-cheir chas-dei a-voht v'i-ma-hoht, u-mei-vi g'u-la li-v'nei v'nei-hem, l'ma-an sh'mo, b'a-ha-va.

BETWEEN ROSH HASHANAH AND YOM KIPPUR ADD:

Zoch'rei-nu l'cha-yim, meh-lech cha-feitz ba-cha-yim, v'cho-t'vei-nu ba-sei-fer ha-cha-yim, l'ma-an-cha Eh-lo-him cha-yim.

Meh-lech o-zeir u-mo-shi-a u-ma-gein.
Ba-ruch a-ta Adonai, ma-gein Av-ra-ham v'ez-rat Sa-rah.

Praised be our God, the God of our fathers and our mothers: God of Abraham, God of Isaac, and God of Jacob; God of Sarah, God of Rebekah, God of Leah and God of Rachel; great, mighty, and awesome God, God supreme.

Ruler of all the living, Your ways are ways of love. You remember the faithfulness of our ancestors, and in love bring redemption to their children's children for the sake of Your name.

BETWEEN ROSH HASHANAH AND YOM KIPPUR ADD:

Remember us unto life, Sovereign who delights in life, and inscribe us in the Book of Life, that Your will may prevail, O God of life.

You are our Sovereign and our Help, our Redeemer and our Shield. We praise You, Eternal One, Shield of Abraham, Protector of Sarah.

GOD'S POWER   גבורות

אַתָּה גִבּוֹר לְעוֹלָם, אֲדֹנָי, מְחַיֵּה הַכֹּל אַתָּה, רַב לְהוֹשִׁיעַ.
מְכַלְכֵּל חַיִּים בְּחֶסֶד, מְחַיֵּה הַכֹּל בְּרַחֲמִים רַבִּים. סוֹמֵךְ
נוֹפְלִים, וְרוֹפֵא חוֹלִים, וּמַתִּיר אֲסוּרִים, וּמְקַיֵּם אֱמוּנָתוֹ
לִישֵׁנֵי עָפָר. מִי כָמוֹךָ בַּעַל גְּבוּרוֹת, וּמִי דוֹמֶה לָךְ, מֶלֶךְ
מֵמִית וּמְחַיֵּה וּמַצְמִיחַ יְשׁוּעָה?

BETWEEN ROSH HASHANAH AND YOM KIPPUR ADD:

מִי כָמוֹךָ, אֵל הָרַחֲמִים, זוֹכֵר יְצוּרָיו לְחַיִּים בְּרַחֲמִים?

וְנֶאֱמָן אַתָּה לְהַחֲיוֹת הַכֹּל. בָּרוּךְ אַתָּה יְיָ, מְחַיֵּה הַכֹּל.

A-ta gi-bor l'o-lam, Adonai, m'cha-yei ha-kol a-ta, rav l'ho-shi-a.
M'chal-keil cha-yim b'cheh-sed, m'cha-yei ha-kol b'ra-cha-mim ra-
bim. So-meich no-f'lim, v'ro-fei cho-lim, u-ma-tir a-su-rim, u-m'ka-
yeim eh-mu-na-toh li-shei-nei a-far. Mi cha-mo-cha ba-al g'vu-roht,
u-mi doh-meh lach, meh-lech mei-mit u-m'cha-yeh u-matz-mi-ach
y'shu-a?

BETWEEN ROSH HASHANAH AND YOM KIPPUR ADD:

Mi cha-mo-cha, eil ha-ra-cha-mim, zo-cheir y'tzu-rav l'cha-yim
b'ra-cha-mim?

V'neh-eh-man a-ta l'ha-cha-yoht ha-kol, Ba-ruch a-ta Adonai,
m'cha-yei ha-kol.

*Eternal is Your might, O God; all life is Your gift; great is
Your power to save!*

*With love You sustain the living, with great compassion
give life to all. You send help to the falling and healing to
the sick; You bring freedom to the captive and keep faith
with those who sleep in the dust.*

*Who is like You, Mighty One? Who is Your equal, Author of
life and death, Source of salvation?*

24

BETWEEN ROSH HASHANAH AND YOM KIPPUR ADD:

Who is like You, Source of mercy?
In compassion You sustain the life of Your children.

We praise You, Eternal God, the Source of life.

THE HOLINESS OF GOD   קדושת השם

אַתָּה קָדוֹשׁ וְשִׁמְךָ קָדוֹשׁ, וּקְדוֹשִׁים בְּכָל־יוֹם יְהַלְלוּךָ סֶּלָה.
בָּרוּךְ* אַתָּה יְיָ, הָאֵל הַקָּדוֹשׁ.

*BETWEEN ROSH HASHANAH AND YOM KIPPUR CONCLUDE:

בָּרוּךְ אַתָּה יְיָ, הַמֶּלֶךְ הַקָּדוֹשׁ.

You are holy, Your name is holy, and those who strive to be holy declare Your glory day by day.

*We praise You, Eternal One, the holy God.

*BETWEEN ROSH HASHANAH AND YOM KIPPUR CONCLUDE:

We praise You, Eternal One: You rule in holiness.

All are seated

(The Intermediate Benedictions, through
page 30, may be recited silently.)

WISDOM   בינה

אַתָּה חוֹנֵן לְאָדָם דַּעַת וּמְלַמֵּד לֶאֱנוֹשׁ בִּינָה. חָנֵּנוּ מֵאִתְּךָ
דֵעָה, בִּינָה וְהַשְׂכֵּל. בָּרוּךְ אַתָּה יְיָ, חוֹנֵן הַדָּעַת.

BY YOUR GRACE we have the power to gain knowledge and to learn wisdom. Favor us with knowledge, wisdom, and insight, for You are their Source.

We praise You, Eternal One, gracious Giver of knowledge.

REPENTANCE   תשובה

הֲשִׁיבֵנוּ אָבִינוּ לְתוֹרָתֶךָ, וְקָרְבֵנוּ מַלְכֵּנוּ לַעֲבוֹדָתֶךָ,
וְהַחֲזִירֵנוּ בִּתְשׁוּבָה שְׁלֵמָה לְפָנֶיךָ. בָּרוּךְ אַתָּה יְיָ,
הָרוֹצֶה בִּתְשׁוּבָה.

HELP US, our Creator, to return to Your Teaching; draw us near,
our Sovereign, to Your service; and bring us back into Your
presence in perfect repentance.

We praise You, Eternal One, who delight in repentance.

FORGIVENESS   סליחה

סְלַח־לָנוּ אָבִינוּ כִּי חָטָאנוּ, מְחַל־לָנוּ מַלְכֵּנוּ כִּי פָשָׁעְנוּ,
כִּי מוֹחֵל וְסוֹלֵחַ אָתָּה. בָּרוּךְ אַתָּה יְיָ, חַנּוּן הַמַּרְבֶּה
לִסְלוֹחַ.

FORGIVE US, our Creator, when we sin; pardon us, our
Sovereign, when we transgress; for You are eager to forgive.

We praise You, Eternal One, gracious and quick to forgive.

REDEMPTION   גאולה

רְאֵה בְעָנְיֵנוּ וְרִיבָה רִיבֵנוּ, וּגְאָלֵנוּ מְהֵרָה לְמַעַן שְׁמֶךָ,
כִּי גוֹאֵל חָזָק אָתָּה. בָּרוּךְ אַתָּה יְיָ, גּוֹאֵל יִשְׂרָאֵל.

LOOK UPON OUR AFFLICTION and help us in our need; O mighty
Redeemer, redeem us speedily for Your name's sake.

We praise You, Eternal One, Redeemer of Israel.

HEALTH   רפואה

רְפָאֵנוּ יְיָ וְנֵרָפֵא, הוֹשִׁיעֵנוּ וְנִוָּשֵׁעָה, וְהַעֲלֵה רְפוּאָה
שְׁלֵמָה לְכָל־מַכּוֹתֵינוּ. בָּרוּךְ אַתָּה יְיָ, רוֹפֵא הַחוֹלִים.

COMPASSIONATE SOURCE OF HEALING, heal us, and we shall be healed; save us, and we shall be saved; grant us a perfect healing for all our infirmities.

(A personal prayer for one who is ill may be added here.)

We praise You, Eternal One, Healer of the sick.

ABUNDANCE   ברכת השים

בָּרֵךְ עָלֵינוּ, יְיָ אֱלֹהֵינוּ, אֶת־הַשָּׁנָה הַזֹּאת וְאֶת־כָּל־מִינֵי
תְבוּאָתָהּ לְטוֹבָה. וְתֵן בְּרָכָה עַל־פְּנֵי הָאֲדָמָה
וְשַׂבְּעֵנוּ מִטּוּבֶךְ. בָּרוּךְ אַתָּה יְיָ, מְבָרֵךְ הַשָּׁנִים.

BLESS THIS YEAR for us, Eternal God: may its produce bring us well-being. Bestow Your blessing on the earth that all Your children may share its abundance in peace.

We praise You, Eternal One, for You bless earth's seasons from year to year.

FREEDOM   חרות

תְּקַע בְּשׁוֹפָר גָּדוֹל לְחֵרוּתֵנוּ, וְשָׂא נֵס לְפְדּוּת עֲשׁוּקֵינוּ,
וְקוֹל דְּרוֹר יִשָּׁמַע בְּאַרְבַּע כַּנְפוֹת הָאָרֶץ.
בָּרוּךְ אַתָּה יְיָ, פּוֹדֶה עֲשׁוּקִים.

SOUND THE GREAT SHOFAR to proclaim freedom, raise high the banner of liberation for the oppressed, and let the song of liberty be heard in the four corners of the earth.

We praise You, Eternal One, Redeemer of the oppressed.

JUSTICE מִשְׁפָּט

עַל שׁוֹפְטֵי אֶרֶץ שְׁפוֹךְ רוּחֶךָ, וְהַדְרִיכֵם בְּמִשְׁפְּטֵי צִדְקֶךָ,
וּמְלוֹךְ עָלֵינוּ אַתָּה לְבַדְּךָ, בְּחֶסֶד וּבְרַחֲמִים.
בָּרוּךְ אַתָּה יְיָ, מֶלֶךְ אוֹהֵב צְדָקָה וּמִשְׁפָּט.

BESTOW YOUR SPIRIT upon the rulers of all lands; guide them,
that they may govern justly. Then shall love and compassion be
enthroned among us.

We praise You, Eternal One, the Sovereign God who loves
righteousness and justice.

ON EVIL עַל הָרִשְׁעָה

וְלָרִשְׁעָה עַל־תְּהִי תִקְוָה, וְהַתּוֹעִים אֵלֶיךָ יָשׁוּבוּ, וּמַלְכוּת
זָדוֹן מְהֵרָה תְשַׁבֵּר. תַּקֵּן מַלְכוּתְךָ בְּתוֹכֵנוּ, בְּקָרוֹב
בְּיָמֵינוּ לְעוֹלָם וָעֶד. בָּרוּךְ אַתָּה יְיָ, הַמַּשְׁבִּית
רֶשַׁע מִן־הָאָרֶץ.

LET THE REIGN OF EVIL afflict us no more. May every errant heart
find its way back to You. O help us to shatter the dominion of
arrogance, to raise up a better world, where virtue will ennoble
the life of Your children.

We praise You, Eternal One, whose will it is that evil vanish
from the earth.

THE RIGHTEOUS עַל הַצַּדִּיקִים

עַל־הַצַּדִּיקִים וְעַל־הַחֲסִידִים וְעַל גֵּרֵי הַצֶּדֶק וְעָלֵינוּ יֶהֱמוּ
רַחֲמֶיךָ, יְיָ אֱלֹהֵינוּ, וְתֵן שָׂכָר טוֹב לְכֹל הַבּוֹטְחִים בְּשִׁמְךָ
בֶּאֱמֶת, וְשִׂים חֶלְקֵנוּ עִמָּהֶם לְעוֹלָם. בָּרוּךְ אַתָּה יְיָ,
מִשְׁעָן וּמִבְטָח לַצַּדִּיקִים.

FOR THE RIGHTEOUS AND FAITHFUL of all humankind, for all who join themselves to our people, for all who put their trust in You, and for all honest men and women, we ask Your favor, Eternal God. Grant that we may always be numbered among them.

We praise You, Eternal One, Staff and Support of the righteous.

JERUSALEM   בונה ירושלים

שְׁכוֹן, יְיָ אֱלֹהֵֽינוּ, בְּתוֹךְ יְרוּשָׁלַֽיִם עִירֶךָ, וִיהִי שָׁלוֹם
בִּשְׁעָרֶֽיהָ, וְשַׁלְוָה בְּלֵב יוֹשְׁבֶֽיהָ, וְתוֹרָתְךָ מִצִּיּוֹן תֵּצֵא,
וּדְבָרְךָ מִירוּשָׁלָֽיִם. בָּרוּךְ אַתָּה יְיָ, בּוֹנֵה יְרוּשָׁלָֽיִם.

LET YOUR PRESENCE be manifest in Jerusalem, Your city. Establish peace in her gates and quietness in the hearts of all who dwell there. Let Your Torah go forth from Zion, Your word from Jerusalem.

We praise You, Eternal One, Builder of Jerusalem.

DELIVERANCE   ישועה

אֶת־צֶֽמַח צְדָקָה מְהֵרָה תַצְמִֽיחַ, וְקֶֽרֶן יְשׁוּעָה תָּרוּם
כִּנְאֻמֶֽךָ, כִּי לִישׁוּעָתְךָ קִוִּֽינוּ כָּל־הַיּוֹם.
בָּרוּךְ אַתָּה יְיָ, מַצְמִֽיחַ קֶֽרֶן יְשׁוּעָה.

LET THE PLANT OF RIGHTEOUSNESS blossom and flourish, and let the light of deliverance shine forth according to Your word: we await Your deliverance all the day.

We praise You, Eternal One, who will cause the light of deliverance to dawn for all the world.

PRAYER   שומע תפלה

שְׁמַע קוֹלֵנוּ, יְיָ אֱלֹהֵינוּ, חוּס וְרַחֵם עָלֵינוּ, וּתְקַבֵּל
בְּרַחֲמִים וּבְרָצוֹן אֶת־תְּפִלָּתֵנוּ, כִּי אֵל שׁוֹמֵעַ תְּפִלוֹת
וְתַחֲנוּנִים אָתָּה. בָּרוּךְ אַתָּה יְיָ, שׁוֹמֵעַ תְּפִלָּה.

HEAR OUR VOICE, ETERNAL GOD; have compassion upon us, and
accept our prayer with favor and mercy, for You are a God who
hears prayer and supplication.

We praise You, Eternal One, who hearkens to prayer.

❖ ❖

WORSHIP   עבודה

רְצֵה, יְיָ אֱלֹהֵינוּ, בְּעַמְּךָ יִשְׂרָאֵל, וּתְפִלָּתָם בְּאַהֲבָה
תְקַבֵּל, וּתְהִי לְרָצוֹן תָּמִיד עֲבוֹדַת יִשְׂרָאֵל עַמֶּךָ.
אֵל קָרוֹב לְכָל־קֹרְאָיו, פְּנֵה אֶל עֲבָדֶיךָ וְחָנֵּנוּ;
שְׁפוֹךְ רוּחֲךָ עָלֵינוּ, וְתֶחֱזֶינָה עֵינֵינוּ בְּשׁוּבְךָ
לְצִיּוֹן בְּרַחֲמִים.
בָּרוּךְ אַתָּה יְיָ, הַמַּחֲזִיר שְׁכִינָתוֹ לְצִיּוֹן.

Be gracious, Eternal God, to Your people Israel, and receive our
prayers with love. O may our worship always be acceptable to
You.

Fill us with the knowledge that You are near to all who
seek You in truth. Let our eyes behold Your presence in our
midst and in the midst of our people in Zion. We praise
You, Eternal One, whose presence gives life to Zion and all
Israel.

ON ROSH CHODESH AND CHOL HAMO-EID :

אֱלֹהֵינוּ וֵאלֹהֵי אֲבוֹתֵינוּ וְאִמּוֹתֵינוּ, יַעֲלֶה וְיָבֹא וְיִזָּכֵר
זִכְרוֹנֵנוּ וְזִכְרוֹן כָּל־עַמְּךָ בֵּית יִשְׂרָאֵל לְפָנֶיךָ לְטוֹבָה
לְחֵן לְחֶסֶד וּלְרַחֲמִים, לְחַיִּים וּלְשָׁלוֹם בְּיוֹם

Our God, God of our fathers and our mothers, be mindful of
Your people Israel on this

- first day of the new month,

•רֹאשׁ הַחֹדֶשׁ הַזֶּה.

- day of Pesach,

•חַג הַמַּצּוֹת הַזֶּה.

- day of Sukkot,

•חַג הַסֻּכּוֹת הַזֶּה.

זָכְרֵנוּ, יְיָ אֱלֹהֵינוּ, בּוֹ לְטוֹבָה. אָמֵן.

וּפָקְדֵנוּ בוֹ לִבְרָכָה. אָמֵן.

וְהוֹשִׁיעֵנוּ בוֹ לְחַיִּים. אָמֵן.

and renew in us love and compassion, goodness, life, and peace.
This day remember us for well-being. *Amen.*
This day bless us with Your nearness. *Amen.*
This day help us to lead a full life. *Amen.*

THANKSGIVING   הודאה

מוֹדִים אֲנַחְנוּ לָךְ, שָׁאַתָּה הוּא יְיָ אֱלֹהֵינוּ וֵאלֹהֵי
אֲבוֹתֵינוּ וְאִמּוֹתֵינוּ לְעוֹלָם וָעֶד. צוּר חַיֵּינוּ, מָגֵן יִשְׁעֵנוּ,
אַתָּה הוּא לְדוֹר וָדוֹר. נוֹדֶה לְךָ וּנְסַפֵּר תְּהִלָּתֶךָ, עַל־
חַיֵּינוּ הַמְּסוּרִים בְּיָדֶךָ, וְעַל־נִשְׁמוֹתֵינוּ הַפְּקוּדוֹת לָךְ,
וְעַל־נִסֶּיךָ שֶׁבְּכָל־יוֹם עִמָּנוּ, וְעַל־נִפְלְאוֹתֶיךָ וְטוֹבוֹתֶיךָ
שֶׁבְּכָל־עֵת, עֶרֶב וָבֹקֶר וְצָהֳרָיִם. הַטּוֹב: כִּי לֹא־כָלוּ
רַחֲמֶיךָ, וְהַמְרַחֵם: כִּי־לֹא תַמּוּ חֲסָדֶיךָ, מֵעוֹלָם קִוִּינוּ
לָךְ. וְעַל כֻּלָּם יִתְבָּרַךְ וְיִתְרוֹמַם שִׁמְךָ, מַלְכֵּנוּ, תָּמִיד
לְעוֹלָם וָעֶד.

BETWEEN ROSH HASHANAH AND YOM KIPPUR ADD:

וּכְתוֹב לְחַיִּים טוֹבִים כָּל־בְּנֵי בְרִיתֶךָ.

וְכֹל הַחַיִּים יוֹדוּךָ סֶּלָה, וִיהַלְלוּ אֶת שִׁמְךָ בֶּאֱמֶת,
הָאֵל יְשׁוּעָתֵנוּ וְעֶזְרָתֵנוּ סֶלָה.
בָּרוּךְ אַתָּה יְיָ, הַטּוֹב שִׁמְךָ וּלְךָ נָאֶה לְהוֹדוֹת.

*We gratefully acknowledge that You are our God and the
God of our people, the God of all the generations. You are
the Rock of our life, the Power that shields us in every age.
We thank You and sing Your praises: for our lives, which
are in Your hand; for our souls, which are in Your keeping;
for the signs of Your presence we encounter every day; and
for Your wondrous gifts at all times, morning, noon, and
night. You are Goodness: Your mercies never end; You are
Compassion: Your love will never fail. You have always
been our hope.*

For all these things, O Sovereign God, let Your name be for ever
exalted and blessed.

BETWEEN ROSH HASHANAH AND YOM KIPPUR ADD:

May all who are loyal to Your covenant
be inscribed for a good life.

O God our Redeemer and Helper, let all who live affirm You
and praise Your name in truth. Eternal God, whose nature is
Goodness, we give You thanks and praise.

ON CHANUKAH ADD:

עַל הַנִּסִּים וְעַל הַפֻּרְקָן, וְעַל הַגְּבוּרוֹת וְעַל הַתְּשׁוּעוֹת,
וְעַל הַמִּלְחָמוֹת, שֶׁעָשִׂיתָ לַאֲבוֹתֵינוּ וּלְאִמּוֹתֵינוּ בַּיָּמִים
הָהֵם בַּזְּמַן הַזֶּה. בִּימֵי מַתִּתְיָהוּ בֶּן־יוֹחָנָן כֹּהֵן גָּדוֹל,
חַשְׁמוֹנַאי וּבָנָיו, כְּשֶׁעָמְדָה מַלְכוּת יָוָן הָרְשָׁעָה עַל עַמְּךָ
יִשְׂרָאֵל, לְהַשְׁכִּיחָם תּוֹרָתֶךָ וּלְהַעֲבִירָם מֵחֻקֵּי רְצוֹנֶךָ.
וְאַתָּה בְּרַחֲמֶיךָ הָרַבִּים עָמַדְתָּ לָהֶם בְּעֵת צָרָתָם, רַבְתָּ
אֶת־רִיבָם, דַּנְתָּ אֶת־דִּינָם, נָקַמְתָּ אֶת־נִקְמָתָם, מָסַרְתָּ
גִבּוֹרִים בְּיַד חַלָּשִׁים, וְרַבִּים בְּיַד מְעַטִּים, וּטְמֵאִים בְּיַד
טְהוֹרִים, וּרְשָׁעִים בְּיַד צַדִּיקִים, וְזֵדִים בְּיַד עוֹסְקֵי
תוֹרָתֶךָ. וּלְךָ עָשִׂיתָ שֵׁם גָּדוֹל וְקָדוֹשׁ בְּעוֹלָמֶךָ, וּלְעַמְּךָ
יִשְׂרָאֵל עָשִׂיתָ תְּשׁוּעָה גְדוֹלָה וּפֻרְקָן כְּהַיּוֹם הַזֶּה. וְאַחַר

כֵּן בָּאוּ בָנֶיךָ לִדְבִיר בֵּיתֶךָ, וּפִנּוּ אֶת־הֵיכָלֶךָ, וְטִהֲרוּ
אֶת־מִקְדָּשֶׁךָ, וְהִדְלִיקוּ נֵרוֹת בְּחַצְרוֹת קָדְשֶׁךָ, וְקָבְעוּ
שְׁמוֹנַת יְמֵי חֲנֻכָּה אֵלּוּ, לְהוֹדוֹת וּלְהַלֵּל לְשִׁמְךָ הַגָּדוֹל.

We give thanks for the redeeming wonders and the mighty deeds
by which at this season our people was saved in days of old.

In the days of the Hasmoneans, a tyrant rose up against our ancestors, determined to make them forget Your Torah, and to turn
them away from obedience to Your will. But You were at their
side in time of trouble. You gave them strength to struggle and
to triumph, that they might serve You in freedom.

Through the power of Your spirit the weak defeated the strong,
the few prevailed over the many, and the righteous were tri-
umphant. Then Your children returned to Your house, to purify
the sanctuary and to kindle its lights. And they dedicated these
days to give thanks and praise to Your great name.

ON PURIM ADD:

עַל הַנִּסִּים וְעַל הַפֻּרְקָן, וְעַל הַגְּבוּרוֹת וְעַל הַתְּשׁוּעוֹת,
וְעַל הַמִּלְחָמוֹת, שֶׁעָשִׂיתָ לַאֲבוֹתֵינוּ וּלְאִמּוֹתֵינוּ בַּיָּמִים הָהֵם
בַּזְּמַן הַזֶּה. בִּימֵי מָרְדְּכַי וְאֶסְתֵּר בְּשׁוּשַׁן הַבִּירָה, כְּשֶׁעָמַד
עֲלֵיהֶם הָמָן הָרָשָׁע, בִּקֵּשׁ לְהַשְׁמִיד לַהֲרֹג וּלְאַבֵּד
אֶת־כָּל־הַיְּהוּדִים, מִנַּעַר וְעַד־זָקֵן, טַף וְנָשִׁים, בְּיוֹם
אֶחָד, בִּשְׁלֹשָׁה עָשָׂר לְחֹדֶשׁ שְׁנֵים־עָשָׂר, הוּא־חֹדֶשׁ
אֲדָר, וּשְׁלָלָם לָבוֹז. וְאַתָּה בְּרַחֲמֶיךָ הָרַבִּים הֵפַרְתָּ
אֶת־עֲצָתוֹ וְקִלְקַלְתָּ אֶת־מַחֲשַׁבְתּוֹ.

We give thanks for the redeeming wonders and the mighty deeds by
which, at this season, our people was saved in days of old.

In the days of Esther and Mordechai, the wicked Haman arose in
Persia, plotting the destruction of all the Jews. He planned to destroy
them in a single day, the thirteenth of Adar, and to permit the
plunder of their possessions.

But through Your great mercy his plan was thwarted, his scheme
frustrated. We therefore thank and praise You, O great and gracious
God!

33

PEACE   ברכת שלום

שָׁלוֹם רָב עַל־יִשְׂרָאֵל עַמְּךָ תָּשִׂים לְעוֹלָם,

כִּי אַתָּה הוּא מֶלֶךְ אָדוֹן לְכָל הַשָּׁלוֹם. וְטוֹב בְּעֵינֶיךָ

לְבָרֵךְ אֶת־עַמְּךָ יִשְׂרָאֵל בְּכָל־עֵת וּבְכָל־שָׁעָה בִּשְׁלוֹמֶךָ.

*בָּרוּךְ אַתָּה יְיָ, הַמְבָרֵךְ אֶת־עַמּוֹ יִשְׂרָאֵל בַּשָּׁלוֹם.

*BETWEEN ROSH HASHANAH AND YOM KIPPUR CONCLUDE:

בְּסֵפֶר חַיִּים וּבְרָכָה נִכָּתֵב לְחַיִּים טוֹבִים וּלְשָׁלוֹם.

בָּרוּךְ אַתָּה יְיָ, עוֹשֵׂה הַשָּׁלוֹם.

*O Sovereign Source of peace, let Israel Your people know
enduring peace, for it is good in Your sight to bless Israel
continually with Your peace.*

* We praise You, Eternal One: You bless Israel with peace.

*BETWEEN ROSH HASHANAH AND YOM KIPPUR CONCLUDE:

Inscribe us in the Book of life, blessing, and peace. We
praise You, Eternal One, the Source of peace.

SILENT PRAYER

אֱלֹהַי, נְצֹר לְשׁוֹנִי מֵרָע, וּשְׂפָתַי מִדַּבֵּר מִרְמָה. וְלִמְקַלְלַי

נַפְשִׁי תִדּוֹם וְנַפְשִׁי כֶּעָפָר לַכֹּל תִּהְיֶה. פְּתַח לִבִּי בְּתוֹרָתֶךָ,

וּבְמִצְוֹתֶיךָ תִּרְדֹּף נַפְשִׁי. וְכָל־הַחוֹשְׁבִים עָלַי רָעָה, מְהֵרָה

הָפֵר עֲצָתָם וְקַלְקֵל מַחֲשַׁבְתָּם. עֲשֵׂה לְמַעַן שְׁמֶךָ, עֲשֵׂה

לְמַעַן יְמִינֶךָ, עֲשֵׂה לְמַעַן קְדֻשָּׁתֶךָ, עֲשֵׂה לְמַעַן תּוֹרָתֶךָ;

לְמַעַן יֵחָלְצוּן יְדִידֶיךָ, הוֹשִׁיעָה יְמִינְךָ וַעֲנֵנִי.

O God, keep my tongue from evil and my lips from deceit. Help
me to be silent in the face of derision, humble in the presence of
all. Open my heart to Your Torah, and I will hasten to do Your
Mitzvot. Save me with Your power; in time of trouble be my
answer, that those who love You may rejoice.

❖ ❖

יִהְיוּ לְרָצוֹן אִמְרֵי־פִי וְהֶגְיוֹן לִבִּי לְפָנֶיךָ, יהוה, צוּרִי וְגֹאֲלִי.

May the words of my mouth, and the meditations of my heart,
be acceptable to You, O God, my Rock and my Redeemer.

❖

עֹשֶׂה שָׁלוֹם בִּמְרוֹמָיו, הוּא יַעֲשֶׂה שָׁלוֹם עָלֵינוּ וְעַל־כָּל־
יִשְׂרָאֵל, וְאִמְרוּ אָמֵן.

O-seh sha-lom bim-ro-mav, hu ya-a-seh sha-lom a-lei-nu v'al kol
Yis-ra-eil, v'im-ru: A-mein.

May the One who causes peace to reign in the high heavens let
peace descend on us, on all Israel, and all the world.

Aleinu is on page 41

A MEDITATION

When we are dead, and people weep for us and grieve, let it be because we touched their lives with beauty and simplicity. Let it not be said that life was good to us, but, rather, that we were good to life.

—*Jacob Philip Rudin*

Days are scrolls; write on them what you want to be remembered.

—*Bachya ibn Pakuda*

At a House of Mourning

We are assembled with our friends in the shadow that has fallen on their home. We raise our voices together in prayer to the Source of life, asking for comfort and strength.

We need light when gloom darkens our home; to whom shall we look, if not to the Creator of light? We need fortitude and courage when pain and loss assail us; where shall we find them, if not in the thought of the One who preserves all that is good from destruction?

Who among us has not passed through trials and bereavements? Some bear fresh wounds in their hearts, and therefore feel more keenly the kinship of sorrow; Others, whose days of mourning are more remote, still recall the comfort that sympathy brought to their sorrowing hearts.

All things pass; all that lives must die. All that we prize is but lent to us, and the time comes when we must surrender it. We are travellers on the same road that leads to the same end.

MEDITATION

As in the world around us, so too in human life: darkness is followed by light, and sorrow by consolation. Life and death are twins; grief and hope walk hand in hand. Although we cannot know what lies beyond the body's death, we put our trust in the undying Spirit that calls us into life and abides to all eternity.

❖ ❖

Eternal God of the spirits of all flesh, You are close to the hearts of the sorrowing, to strengthen and console them with the warmth of Your love, and with the assurance that the human spirit is enduring and indestructible. Even as we pray for perfect peace for those whose lives have ended, so do we ask You to give comfort and courage to the living.

May the knowledge of Your nearness be our strength, O God, for You are with us at all times: in joy and sorrow, in light and darkness, in life and death.

אָנָּא, יְיָ, הָרוֹפֵא לִשְׁבוּרֵי לֵב וּמְחַבֵּשׁ לְעַצְּבוֹתָם, שַׁלֵּם
נֶחוּמִים לָאֲבֵלִים. חַזְּקֵם וְאַמְּצֵם בְּיוֹם אֶבְלָם וִיגוֹנָם,
וְזָכְרֵם לְחַיִּים טוֹבִים וַאֲרֻכִּים.
תֵּן בְּלִבָּם יִרְאָתְךָ וְאַהֲבָתְךָ לְעָבְדְּךָ בְּלֵבָב שָׁלֵם.
וּתְהִי אַחֲרִיתָם שָׁלוֹם. אָמֵן.

O God, Healer of the broken-hearted and Binder of their wounds, grant consolation to those who mourn. Give them strength and courage in the time of their grief, and restore to them a sense of life's goodness.

Fill them with reverence and love, that they may serve You with a whole heart, and let them soon know peace. Amen.

Psalm 23

מִזְמוֹר לְדָוִד.
יהוה רֹעִי, לֹא אֶחְסָר. בִּנְאוֹת דֶּשֶׁא יַרְבִּיצֵנִי,
עַל־מֵי מְנֻחוֹת יְנַהֲלֵנִי. נַפְשִׁי יְשׁוֹבֵב,
יַנְחֵנִי בְמַעְגְּלֵי־צֶדֶק לְמַעַן שְׁמוֹ.
גַּם כִּי־אֵלֵךְ בְּגֵיא צַלְמָוֶת לֹא־אִירָא רָע,
כִּי־אַתָּה עִמָּדִי: שִׁבְטְךָ וּמִשְׁעַנְתֶּךָ, הֵמָּה יְנַחֲמֻנִי.
תַּעֲרֹךְ לְפָנַי שֻׁלְחָן נֶגֶד צֹרְרָי,
דִּשַּׁנְתָּ בַשֶּׁמֶן רֹאשִׁי, כּוֹסִי רְוָיָה.

אַךְ טוֹב וָחֶסֶד יִרְדְּפוּנִי כָּל־יְמֵי חַיָּי,
וְשַׁבְתִּי בְּבֵית־יהוה לְאֹרֶךְ יָמִים.

A Song of David.
Eternal One, You are my shepherd, I shall not want. You make me lie down in green pastures, You lead me beside still waters. You restore my soul; You guide me in paths of righteousness for Your name's sake. Even when I walk through the valley of the shadow of death, I will fear no evil, for You are with me; with rod and staff You comfort me. You prepare a table before me in the presence of my enemies; You have anointed my head with oil; my cup is overflowing. Surely, goodness and mercy shall follow me all the days of my life, and I shall dwell in Your house for ever.

❖ ❖

At this hour, especially, the blessed presence of family and friends brings us comfort and strength. It says to us: "Be sure that love, the spring of life, abides."

May all who mourn take heart, as they remember the goodness they have given and received. And when the days of their mourning are ended, may the memory of their loved ones come to be a benediction.

בָּרוּךְ אַתָּה יְיָ, מְחַיֵּה הַכֹּל.

Ba-ruch a-ta Adonai, m'cha-yei ha-kol.

Praised be the Eternal Source of life.

❖ ❖

All rise

אֵל מָלֵא רַחֲמִים, שׁוֹכֵן בַּמְּרוֹמִים, הַמְצֵא מְנוּחָה נְכוֹנָה
תַּחַת כַּנְפֵי הַשְּׁכִינָה עִם קְדוֹשִׁים וּטְהוֹרִים כְּזֹהַר
הָרָקִיעַ מַזְהִירִים אֶת נִשְׁמַת . . . שֶׁהָלַךְ לְעוֹלָמוֹ
(שֶׁהָלְכָה לְעוֹלָמָהּ). בַּעַל הָרַחֲמִים יַסְתִּירֵהוּ (יַסְתִּירֶהָ)
בְּסֵתֶר כְּנָפָיו לְעוֹלָמִים. וְיִצְרוֹר בִּצְרוֹר הַחַיִּים אֶת ־
נִשְׁמָתוֹ (נִשְׁמָתָהּ). יְיָ הוּא נַחֲלָתוֹ (נַחֲלָתָהּ) וְיָנוּחַ
(וְתָנוּחַ) בְּשָׁלוֹם עַל מִשְׁכָּבוֹ (מִשְׁכָּבָהּ), וְנֹאמַר: אָמֵן.

God full of compassion, You dwell in the heights and in the
depths: grant perfect rest under the wings of Your Presence to...
our loved one who has entered eternity. Let her/him find refuge
for ever in the shadow of Your wings, and let her/his soul be
bound up in the bond of eternal life; for You, the Everlasting
God, are her/his inheritance. May she/he rest in peace, and let us
say: *Amen.*

Aleinu

עָלֵינוּ

All rise

עָלֵינוּ לְשַׁבֵּחַ לַאֲדוֹן הַכֹּל, לָתֵת גְּדֻלָּה לְיוֹצֵר בְּרֵאשִׁית,
שֶׁלֹּא עָשָׂנוּ כְּגוֹיֵי הָאֲרָצוֹת, וְלֹא שָׂמָנוּ כְּמִשְׁפְּחוֹת
הָאֲדָמָה; שֶׁלֹּא שָׂם חֶלְקֵנוּ כָּהֶם, וְגוֹרָלֵנוּ כְּכָל־הֲמוֹנָם.

וַאֲנַחְנוּ כּוֹרְעִים וּמִשְׁתַּחֲוִים וּמוֹדִים לִפְנֵי
מֶלֶךְ מַלְכֵי הַמְּלָכִים, הַקָּדוֹשׁ בָּרוּךְ הוּא.

A-lei-nu l'sha-bei-ach la-a-don ha-kol, la-teit g'du-la l'yo-tzeir b'rei-shit, sheh-lo a-sa-nu k'go-yei ha-a-ra-tzot, v'lo sa-ma-nu k'mish-p'choht ha-a-da-ma; sheh-lo sam chel-kei-nu ka-hem, v'go-ra-lei-nu k'chol ha-mo-nam.

Va-a-nach-nu kor-im u-mish-ta-cha-vim u-mo-dim lif-nei meh-lech mal-chei ha-m'la-chim, ha-ka-dosh ba-ruch hu.

°We praise the One who gave us life. In our rejoicing You are God; You are God in our grief. In anguish and deliverance alike, we praise; in darkness and light we affirm our faith. Therefore we bow our heads in reverence before the Eternal God of life, the Holy One, the Blessed One.

Eternal God, we face the morrow with hope made stronger by the vision of Your deliverance, a world where poverty and war are banished, where injustice and hate are gone.

Teach us more and more to respond to the pain of others, to heed Your call for justice, to pursue the blessing of peace. And grant us wisdom and strength, O God, that we may bring nearer the day when all the world shall be one.

On that day the age-old hope shall come true. On that day, O God, You shall be One and Your name shall be One.

וְנֶאֱמַר: "וְהָיָה יהוה לְמֶלֶךְ עַל־כָּל־הָאָרֶץ; בַּיוֹם הַהוּא יִהְיֶה יהוה אֶחָד וּשְׁמוֹ אֶחָד."

V'neh-eh-mar: "V'ha-ya Adonai l'meh-lech al kol ha-a-retz;
ba-yom ha-hu yi-h'yeh Adonai eh-chad, u-sh'mo eh-chad!"

And it has been said: "The Eternal God shall rule over all the earth; On that day You shall be One and Your name shall be One."

Before the Kaddish

WHEN CHERISHED TIES are broken, and the chain of love is shattered, only trust and the strength of faith can lighten the heaviness of the heart. At times, the pain of separation seems more than we can bear; but love and understanding can help us pass through the darkness toward the light.

Out of affliction the Psalmist learned the law of God. And in truth, grief is a great teacher, when it sends us back to serve and bless the living. We learn how to counsel and comfort those who, like ourselves, are bowed with sorrow. We learn when to keep silence in their presence, and when a word will assure them of our love and concern.

Thus, even when they are gone, the departed are with us, moving us to live as, in their higher moments, they themselves wished to live. We remember them now; they live in our hearts; they are an abiding blessing.

Mourner's Kaddish   קדיש יתום

יִתְגַּדַּל וְיִתְקַדַּשׁ שְׁמֵהּ רַבָּא בְּעָלְמָא דִּי־בְרָא כִרְעוּתֵהּ,
וְיַמְלִיךְ מַלְכוּתֵהּ בְּחַיֵּיכוֹן וּבְיוֹמֵיכוֹן וּבְחַיֵּי דְכָל־בֵּית
יִשְׂרָאֵל, בַּעֲגָלָא וּבִזְמַן קָרִיב, וְאִמְרוּ: אָמֵן.

Yit-ga-dal v'yit-ka-dash sh'mei ra-ba b'al-ma di-v'ra chir-u-tei,
v'yam-lich mal-chu-tei b'cha-yei-chon u-v'yo-mei-chon u-v'cha-yei
d'chol beit Yis-ra-eil, ba-a-ga-la u-viz-man ka-riv, v'im-ru: A-mein.

יְהֵא שְׁמֵהּ רַבָּא מְבָרַךְ לְעָלַם וּלְעָלְמֵי עָלְמַיָּא.

Y'hei sh'mei ra-ba m'va-rach l'a-lam u-l'al-mei al-ma-ya.

43

יִתְבָּרַךְ וְיִשְׁתַּבַּח, וְיִתְפָּאַר וְיִתְרוֹמַם וְיִתְנַשֵּׂא, וְיִתְהַדָּר
וְיִתְעַלֶּה וְיִתְהַלַּל שְׁמֵהּ דְּקֻדְשָׁא, בְּרִיךְ הוּא,

Yit-ba-rach v'yish-ta-bach v'yit-pa-ar, v'yit-ro-mam, v'yit-na-sei,
v'yit-ha-dar, v'yit-a-leh, v'yit-ha-lal sh'mei d'kud'sha, b'rich hu,

לְעֵלָּא מִן־כָּל־בִּרְכָתָא וְשִׁירָתָא, תֻּשְׁבְּחָתָא וְנֶחֱמָתָא
דַּאֲמִירָן בְּעָלְמָא, וְאִמְרוּ: אָמֵן.

L'ei-la min kol bir-cha-ta v'shi-ra-ta, tush-b'cha-ta v'neh-cheh-ma-ta
da-a-mi-ran b'al-ma, v'im-ru: A-mein.

יְהֵא שְׁלָמָא רַבָּא מִן־שְׁמַיָּא וְחַיִּים עָלֵינוּ וְעַל־כָּל־
יִשְׂרָאֵל, וְאִמְרוּ: אָמֵן.

Y'hei sh'la-ma ra-ba min sh'ma-ya v'cha-yim, a-lei-nu v'al kol
Yis-ra-eil, v'im-ru: A-mein.

עֹשֶׂה שָׁלוֹם בִּמְרוֹמָיו, הוּא יַעֲשֶׂה שָׁלוֹם עָלֵינוּ וְעַל־כָּל־
יִשְׂרָאֵל, וְאִמְרוּ: אָמֵן.

O-seh sha-lom bim-ro-mav, hu ya-a-seh sha-lom a-lei-nu v'al kol
Yis-ra-eil, v'im-ru: A-mein.

Let the glory of God be extolled, and God's great name be hallowed in the
world whose creation God willed. May God rule in our own day, in our
own lives, and in the life of all Israel, and let us say: Amen.

Let God's great name be blessed for ever and ever.

Beyond all the praises, songs, and adorations that we can utter is the Holy
One, the Blessed One, whom yet we glorify, honor, and exalt. And let us
say: Amen.

For us and for all Israel, may the blessing of peace and the promise of life
come true, and let us say: Amen.

May the One who causes peace to reign in the high heavens, let peace
descend on us, on all Israel, and all the world, and let us say: Amen.

❖

May the Source of peace send peace to all who mourn, and comfort to all who are bereaved. *Amen.*